Trouble at Sea

Written by

Rob Waring and **Maurice Jamall**

(with contributions by **Julian Thomlinson**)

Before You Read

to swim

barrel

bird

dead
(to die)

dolphin

fish

head

hill

hotel

land

oil

rocks

sea

In the story

David

Faye

Tyler

John

Daniela

Mr. Jenkins

"Where do you want to swim today?" asked Faye.
It was another hot day in Bayview. Faye and her friends
put all their things in the boat. They were ready to go!
"Let's go to Jenkins Cove," said Tyler. He was pointing
at an old house on the hill. "It's always a good place to
swim. Maybe we can see some dolphins."
"Yeah. Good idea. Let's go there," said the others.

Faye drove the boat into Jenkins Cove. She loved driving the boat. John pointed at the house on the hill. "Look! Is that Mr. Jenkins's house?" he asked. "Yes. I think so," said David, sitting at the front of the boat. Mr. Jenkins was their friend. They often went to his house. Daniela wasn't listening, she was taking pictures. "Smile, Faye," Daniela said to her friend.

In Jenkins Cove, they saw a boat. It was a very big and very expensive boat.

David pointed at the boat and said, "Wow! Look at that boat. Isn't it beautiful?"

"Now that's a *real* boat," said John. "Not like our small one. I want that kind of boat one day. It looks great."

They all loved the boat. "I want to go on it," said Daniela. They looked at the boat for a long time.

They stopped their boat near some rocks.

"I'm going in," said John. "How about you, David? Are you coming in?" he asked.

"Yes. I'm coming," said David. "Daniela, are you coming?" he asked.

"Umm . . . No, thanks," she said. "It looks too cold for me!"

Tyler said, "No, thanks. I want to fish."

Faye was getting ready to go in the water, too. "I'll come with you," said Faye. "I want to swim, too."

They all got ready. Tyler started to fish and the others started to put on their swimming things. Then David looked out at sea. "What's that?" he asked. He pointed at something in the water. "What's what?" asked Daniela.

"There! There's something in the water. It's moving. Let's go and see it," said David.

They all looked at it. "What is it?" asked Daniela.
David said, "Oh no! It's a bird. It's covered in black oil."
"Who would do such a terrible thing?" asked Faye. "Who would put oil in the sea?"
"I don't know," replied John. "But I don't like them at all."
David picked up the bird and put it in the boat. They all looked at the small bird.

"Will it live?" asked Daniela.

"I don't know," replied David. "It's covered in oil, so it can't fly or eat. We have to clean it, or it'll die."

John asked, "David, you're good with animals. Can you help it?"

"No, I can't. But I think Mr. Jenkins can," he replied. "He works at Bayview Zoo. Let's go and see him."

They all agreed, and Faye drove the boat back to the beach.
They wanted to find Mr. Jenkins.

Everyone was very worried about the bird. They looked everywhere for Mr. Jenkins. At last, they found him. He was on the beach, standing in the sea with a family of dolphins. David and the others ran quickly to him. "Mr. Jenkins!" shouted David. "Mr. Jenkins!" But he did not look at David and the others.

Mr. Jenkins did not look happy. He looked very angry. He looked worried, too. One of the dolphins was sick. There was oil all over the dolphin's head. Its head was black from the oil. Mr. Jenkins was washing the oil off the dolphin.

"Who did this to you?" Mr. Jenkins asked the dolphin. "This is so bad. There is so much oil everywhere." The other dolphins watched as Mr. Jenkins cleaned the dolphin.

Mr. Jenkins turned around and looked at David. He saw the bird. "Hello, everybody. Oh no. Not another one!" he said. "Please help. Help the bird, Mr. Jenkins," said David. He showed the bird to Mr. Jenkins. "Will the bird be okay? Will it live?" David asked.

"I don't know. It'll take weeks before the bird is well again. Help me, David," he said. "If you wash the bird, I'll hold it." After they finished washing the bird, Mr. Jenkins said, "I'll take the bird to my house and look after it."

Later, David and the others went out in their boat again.
"Maybe there are some more sick birds," said Daniela.
"I hope not! I hope we don't find any more," said Faye.
Tyler took their boat out into Jenkins Cove.
"Let's go swimming," said John. "I want to forget about
that bird."
"That's a good idea," said Daniela. "It's a good day for
swimming."
But David was quiet. "Oh, no!" he said. "Oh no!"

All around the boat were dead fish and dead birds. Oil was everywhere.

"No! I can't believe this," said Daniela. "Look at these poor things. It's so sad."

David was very shocked, too. He could not speak. He loved animals and hated to see them in the oil. He started to cry.

"Who put the oil in the sea?" asked John.

"I don't know, but we must stop them," replied Faye. "All the fish and birds will die if we don't stop these people."

Tyler saw the big boat again. The oil was coming from the boat.
"Look! The oil is coming from that boat. They're putting the oil
in the water," said Tyler. "Let's go and stop them!"
Everyone agreed to go to the big boat.
"But let's be careful," said Faye. "We have to find out *why*
they're putting oil in the sea."
"Good idea, Faye," said Daniela. "Let's go quietly and listen to
them."

Slowly and quietly, they took their small boat nearer to the big boat. They could see the men on the boat. They were putting oil into the sea from big barrels.

"Look at that! Can you see? They're putting oil into the sea!" said David quietly.

"We were right!" said John. "It *was* them. So what are we going to do?"

Faye said, "I'm going to swim up to the boat and listen to the men. I want to find out why they are doing this. Who's coming with me?"

"I'll come with you," said Tyler.

Faye and Tyler went quietly into the water. They did not want the men to see or hear them. They swam to the boat. They could not see the men, but they could hear them. They listened carefully.

One man said, "Carlos, can you see any other boats?"

The man replied, "No, Jim. Nobody's watching. Let's finish this quickly."

"The men are talking," Faye said quietly to Tyler. "Let's go and listen to them." They took their small boat nearer to the big boat.

Tyler and Faye listened to the men from the water. They could hear the men talking about the house on the hill. A big man in white was pointing to it.

"Carlos," said Jim, the man in red, "putting the oil in the sea was a good idea. It'll stop people coming to this beach." Carlos replied, "Yes, the beach will be bad for two or three years, and the people will stop coming."

"So then we can buy that house cheaply," said his friend.

"When the water becomes clean again, we can build our big hotel there!" The men laughed.

"Faye, they're talking about Mr. Jenkins's house!" said Tyler quietly. "They want to buy it!"
"Yes, I heard," she replied. "They're killing the fish and birds because they want to build a hotel! That's terrible!"
They listened to the men again. Carlos spoke again.
"Yes, it's a great plan!" said Carlos. "And then we'll be rich. Very rich!"
Faye and Tyler heard the men. "They can't do that! Let's go back to the boat and tell the police," said Tyler quietly.

Tyler and Faye swam back to the boat. They tried to be quiet so the men could not hear them. John helped Faye get into the boat. Suddenly, Daniela's phone rang. Everyone looked at it! "Oh, no! My phone! My phone!" thought Daniela. "The men will hear that." Her face turned very red.

The men heard the phone. "What was that?" asked Jim.

"It's somebody's phone. It came from over there," replied Carlos. They ran to the side of the boat.

Tyler and Faye heard Daniela's phone ring, too. They could hear the angry men. They did not want the men to see them. They swam next to the big boat.

Jim saw their boat first. "Hey, you! What are you doing here?" shouted Jim. He was very angry.

Everyone was frightened. "Umm . . . We're swimming," said John.

"Well, don't swim near here," replied Jim. "Go away!

"Go away! We don't want you here," said Carlos.
"Yes, we know," said David. He was very angry with the men. "We know your plan to buy the old house and build a hotel. We heard you. And we saw you put oil in the sea. We're going to tell the police."
Carlos said, "Go away! I don't care about the birds and fish. The police won't believe you. We'll say we didn't do it."

Daniela had an idea. She looked at her phone in her hand. Her phone had a camera. She took some pictures of the men and the oil.

"But the police will believe these pictures!" said Daniela. Daniela took many pictures of the boat, the men, and the oil. The men saw Daniela taking pictures.

"Stop her! Get that camera!" said Carlos. "Quick! Start the engine. We have to stop them!"

The men ran to start the boat.

Tyler and Faye also saw Daniela take the pictures.
"Quick, Faye. Let's get back in the boat," said Tyler.
The men then saw Tyler and Faye. "Look! There are five
of them! There are two more in the water," said Carlos.
"Let's get out of here!" said John. He started the boat
engine. "Quick! Faye, Tyler, get in the boat. I'll drive."
"There's no time," said Faye. "You go. We'll swim to the
beach. Get away quickly!"
"No," said Daniela. "David, throw that rope to Faye and
Tyler." David threw a rope to them. John started to drive
the boat back to the beach.

But the rope missed! Faye and Tyler could not get back in the boat. "It's okay!" called Tyler. "We can swim to the beach. Go!"
"Okay, we'll see you at the beach," said John.
"No," said Daniela. "No! The men in the boat will catch you. Swim to the boat. Quickly!"
The big boat started to follow the little boat. Faye and Tyler swam to the small boat. But the big boat was coming to Tyler and Faye fast.

The big boat moved very fast through the water. The men wanted the pictures. The small boat was slow and soon the big boat was near them. Carlos was driving the boat.

"The boat's coming at us," shouted Daniela. She was very frightened.

"Stop! Give me the pictures," shouted Carlos. "Stop, or we'll hit your boat!"

"They're going to hit us!" said John.

Carlos drove the boat very fast. He wanted to hit the small boat. He did not care about Faye or Tyler.

"Look out!" said Jim to Carlos. "There are people in the water!" Carlos did not listen. He wanted the camera. He wanted the pictures. The big boat drove over Tyler and Faye. Carlos laughed.

"Now give me the pictures, or I'll hit your boat, too."

Daniela screamed! "He killed Tyler and Faye!" she screamed. "Where are they?"

John turned the boat away just in time. The big boat missed the small boat.

Suddenly, the dolphins came. One dolphin jumped at Carlos. He was very frightened. More dolphins came and hit the boat. They hit the boat hard many times. Carlos was not laughing now. The dolphins were really angry. "What? What's happening?" shouted Jim. "What are the dolphins doing? What's wrong with the dolphins?"

Then many more dolphins came. They jumped over the boat. One of the barrels hit Benny. The oil went all over the boat. And it went all over the men. One of the men fell into the sea.

"Help!" said the man. "Help!"

The dolphins put water all over the boat. The men did not want to fight the dolphins. Angry dolphins can be very dangerous! The men were very frightened now.

Carlos did not see the rocks. He was looking at the dolphins.
"Look out!" said Jim. "We're going to hit the rocks!"
But Carlos could not stop the big boat in time. The boat hit
the rocks with a big CRASH! Jim fell into the water. Now the
boat had a big hole in it and water was coming into the
boat. The dolphins stopped the men.

Soon the police came. David told the police officer about the men. David told him about the oil, the fish, and the birds and the men's plans. The police took the men off the boat. Everybody on the beach watched the men.

"But what about Faye and Tyler?" asked Daniela.

"We have to look for them." She was very worried about them.

"Let's go and look for them," said John.

Just then there was a noise in the water. The dolphins were bringing Faye and Tyler back to the beach. They were okay. "You're okay!" said Daniela. She ran into the water to meet them. "What happened?" she asked.

Tyler said, "When the boat came for us, we went under the water, so the boat missed us. The dolphins found us and brought us back to the beach. Dolphins are very smart."

"I know," said Mr. Jenkins. "My friends thought you needed some help."